Rue Des Bergers Nature Reserve

Despite its small size, over 300 species of birds have been recorded in the Bailiwick of Guernsey and anyone who goes bird-watching regularly may reasonably expect to see 150 species or more during a single year. However, many people only have a passing interest in birds and are content when they know the identity of a handful of birds visiting the garden.

The aim of this little book is to provide information on Guernsey's most common birds, rather than the rare and unusual ones. With nearly 100 species covered, most of the everyday species are included in order to provide an introduction into the Bailiwick's birdlife.

When I hear local people discussing birds they have seen there is often some confusion. Was it a Sparrowhawk or a Kestrel? Was it a Cormorant or a Shag? Or was that flash of blue really a Kingfisher – we don't get them in Guernsey?! Hopefully this book will help settle at least some of these debates.

For those readers who subsequently find themselves out bird-watching, a more comprehensive field guide of British and European species will soon be required. For most people though, this book will prove to be very handy if kept in the car or on the window sill. Likewise, visitors who are looking for a snapshot of Guernsey's birds will find this a useful starting point.

Happy bird watching!
Jamie Hooper
La Société Guernesiaise Conservation Officer

How many times have you been out walking and seen an interesting bird, but were unable to identify it?

This handy pocket guide to the birds of Guernsey and the Bailiwick is for the serious ornithologist and the keen amateur birdwatcher alike. It is designed to be carried with you whenever you are out walking around the islands. There is a simple description and colour photograph for each entry to make it easy to identify the birds most common to these islands. There is also a list of less common species and occasional visitors.

At the beginning of the book is a list of official bird hides and nature reserves where you can observe a wide range of birds. There is a brief description of the site and simple maps to help you find your way, either by foot, car or via the excellent local bus service.

Guernsey and the islands of the Bailiwick boast a wide variety of resident and migratory bird species and provide an ideal migration stop-off point. The mild winters also make it attractive to birds seeking warmth and food away from the mainland. For such a small land mass the islands offer a wide range of habitats that provide both visitors and locals alike with the perfect opportunity to enjoy a great variety of bird life. Tranquil, low lying wetland areas, dramatic, rugged cliffs and extensive shorelines can all be explored in one day making Guernsey and the other islands of the Bailiwick an ideal place for bird watching.

Guernsey Locations

These sites are all owned or managed by La Société Guernesiaise.

1 La Claire Mare

There are two public hides overlooking a scrape dug into the reed bed. Both can be reached down a drive which runs between the houses on Route De La Rocque, St Saviours.

2 Colin Best Nature Reserve

An adjacent wetland meadow, with a public hide down a track off the Route De La Rocque. Nearby, there are several spaces for car parking for both sites or take the bus on route 7/7.a.

3 Rue Des Bergers

There are two hides on the corner of Rue Des Bergers in the Kings Mills area (at the back of the Fleur du Jardin Hotel). Both overlook a pond and a reed bed lined by trees. Rue Des Bergers is a narrow lane designated as a Ruettes Tranquilles. There is no official car park close by, but the 5/5a bus route runs along the Kings Mills Road. Stop at the Fleur du Jardin Hotel.

4 Vale Pond
(Colin McCathie Nature Reserve)

The entrance to this hide is easily found through a granite wall on La Route De L'Islet, opposite a beach kiosk and large car park. This is an important wetland site of pond, reed bed and meadow. The water can be slightly brackish following high spring tides. Bus route 6/6a and 7/7a (summer only)

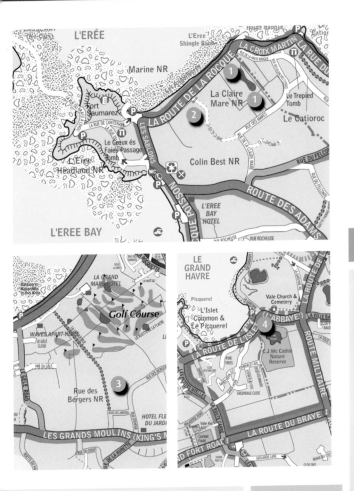

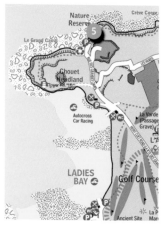

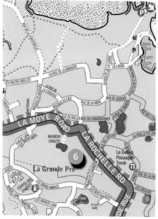

5 Sea watching hide at Chouet
Excellent sea bird watching site at the back of the island's landfill and recycling site. There is parking next to the beach kiosk nearby on Mont Cuet Road. The bus routes 6/6a and 7/7a (summer only) run by the end of Mont Cuet Road.

6 Le Grand Pré - L'Ancresse wetland
This meadow site has the largest reed bed on the island. The site has recently undergone remedial work and there is a new hide. Access to the site is gained via La Blanche Charriere. Alternatively, take the bus route 6/6a

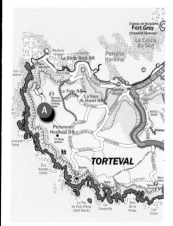

Pleinmont

An area of wild cliff top in the SW tip of the island surrounded by spectacular seas. Contains rough patches of gorse scrub, maritime heathland and arable strip fields. The area is criss-crossed by paths and small narrow lanes. There are numerous car parking places in the area. This is also the bus stop for the route 7/7a.

The Silbe Nature Reserve

Owned by La Société Guernesiaise. This is a small wooded site on the Rue de Quanteraine, St Peters. There is no official car park but the bus route 5/5a runs close by on the Rue De L'Eglise.

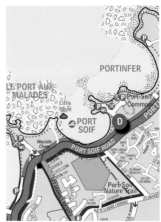

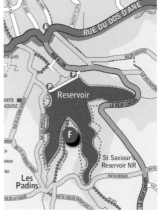

C Belle Greve Bay

The road running north out of St Peter Port around Belle Greve Bay is one of the busiest on the island but it is a rich site for shore birds. From the bay there is a splendid view of Herm, Jethou and Sark. There is parking at La Salerie, the Halfway and Richmond Corner and bus route 8/8a runs along the length of the bay.

D Port Soif

The nature trail and reserve straddles the Port Soif Road in the Vale parish. Follow the path around the bay and cross the road to the sign posted nature trail. There is ample parking on the headland close to the beach kiosk and bus routes 3/3a and 7/7a run along Port Soif Road.

E Fort Hommet Headland

This busy headland site is located at the northern end of Vazon Bay off Rue D'Albecq, Castel. The area comprises scrub, rocky outcrops and beach. The area is popular in summer and surfers enjoy the waves all year round. There is good car parking and the area is served by the 3/3a and 7/7a bus route.

F The Reservoir

The Reservoir, in the parish of St Saviours, is the largest area of freshwater on the island. There is a 3 km path around the Reservoir, known as the 'Millennium Walk', that winds through reed beds and broadleaf and coniferous woodland. There is car parking at either end of the dam, accessible from either Rue a L'Or or Rue Des Annevilles. The nearest bus route is the 5/5a. Stop at Le Mont Saint and walk up Rue a L'Or.

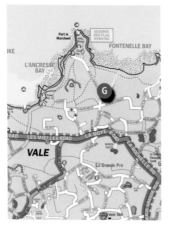

G L'Ancresse Common

The common covers a large area in the north of the island and is popular with golfers, walkers and holidaymakers. The area includes dunes, scrub, gorse and bushes laced with rocky outcrops and rough grassland. Around the beach are rocky headlands. There are several car parks around the coast and the area is served by the 6/6a and 7/7a (summer only) bus routes.

H Vazon Bay

The southern end of the bay, away from the surfers, is an excellent site for wading birds. Parking is available all along the bay. The 7/7a bus route runs the length of the bay.

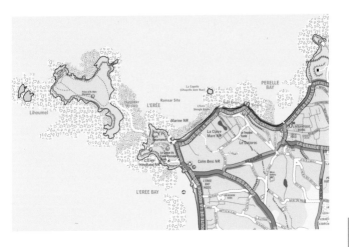

Ramsar Site

Guernsey's first Ramsar site includes Lihou Island, Les Anguillieres Shingle Bank, La Claire Mare Nature Reserve, and the Colin Best Nature Reserve, as well as the intertidal area and outlying reefs and rocks. There is a 4.3 km circular walk which encompasses these important sites, starting at the public car park at L'Eree. There are several parking places around the area and it can be reached by the 5/5a and 7/7a buses. Lihou Island is only accessible at low tide when the causeway is open. Please check local information before crossing.

Herm

Sark

Herm

The lovely island of Herm is an ideal bird watching site and is only a 20 minute ferry ride from St Peter Port. This small island, just 2 sq km in size, is surrounded by spectacular beaches and craggy cliffs. There are rocky out crops, woodlands, fields and a large common. In spring and autumn you can observe a wide variety of migrant birds and there are regular organised birdwatching boat trips around the island.

Sark

Sark is larger than Herm and has a permanent population of over 500 inhabitants. The island is mainly plateau above steep cliffs which encompass the whole coastline. The habitat includes open farmland, deciduous woodland and small areas of scrub and gorse. There is a regular 45 minute ferry connecting Sark to Guernsey throughout the year although the service is limited during the winter.

Alderney

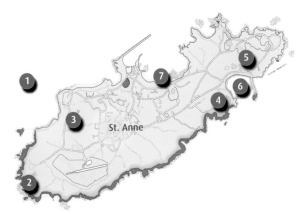

Alderney

Alderney is 5.6 km long and 2.4 km at its widest point. The island lies 37 km north east of Guernsey and only 13 km from the Normandy coast. The island is internationally known for the Gannet colonies found on Ortac and Les Etacs (Garden Rocks) off Giffoine point. For general birdwatching, sites of interest include the Bonne Terre Valley and Barrack Masters Lane, the reed beds around Longis Ponds (where there is a bird hide) and the coastal areas of Longis Bay and Braye Bay. There are regular flights from Guernsey and Southampton.

1. Ortac (5km West of Alderney)
2. Les Etacs
3. Bonne Terre Valley
4. Barracks Masters Lane
5. Longis Ponds
6. Longis Bay
7. Braye Bay

Great Crested Grebe *Podiceps cristatus*

FACT FILE

Common Name:	Great Crested Grebe
Latin Name:	Podiceps cristatus
Identification:	Length 48 cm. Brown black with slender white neck, dark horns and reddish black side frills.
Voice:	Mainly barking or quacking sounds when breeding and normally silent in winter.
Local Status:	Small numbers over winter around the coast.

FACT FILE

Common Name:	Little Grebe
Latin Name:	Tachybaptus ruficollis
Identification:	Length 27 cm. Tiny grebe mainly dark with chestnut cheeks and throat with yellow spot at the base of a small bill.
Voice:	High loud trilling call often rising and falling but normally silent outside of the breeding season.
Local Status:	Mainly seen at St Saviours Reservoir and other larger bodies of fresh water.

Fulmar *Fulmarus glacialis*

FACT FILE

Common Name:	Fulmar
Latin Name:	Fulmarus glacialis
Identification:	Length 47 cm. Gull like but with a bull neck. Grey above and white below with dark eyes and narrow wings.
Voice:	Various chuckling notes and guttural cackling on the nest. Normally silent away from the breeding grounds.
Local Status:	Commonly seen out at sea with a scattered breeding population on local cliffs.

Gannet *Morus bassanus*

FACT FILE

Common Name: Gannet

Latin Name: Morus bassanus

Identification: Length 90 cm. Vary large seabird, cigar shaped with broad narrow wings with a 1.8m wingspan. White with a pale yellow head and black wingtips and is a spectacular flier.

Voice: Gutteral rasps and cries at breeding grounds.

Local Status: Can be seen offshore around Guernsey and two large colonies can be found on Les Etacs and Ortac, small rocky islands off the Alderney coast.

FACT FILE

Common Name:	Cormorant
Latin Name:	Phalacrocorax carbo
Identification:	Length 90 cm. Black and dark brown above and glossy blue black below with white chin and white thigh patch when breeding.
Voice:	Hoarse croaking and growling at the nest, otherwise mainly silent.
Local Status:	Found in various coastal locations, ponds and reservoirs.

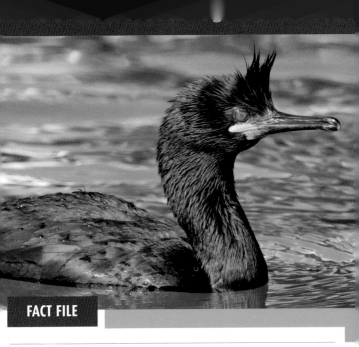

FACT FILE

Common Name:	Shag
Latin Name:	Phalacrocorax aristotelis
Identification:	Length 76 cm. Slimmer than the cormorant, glossy green black with a yellow gape and in spring an upright crest.
Voice:	Guttural croaking during breeding time, otherwise silent.
Local Status:	A very common marine species found all around the coast.

Little Egret *Egretta garzetta*

FACT FILE

Common Name: Little Egret

Latin Name: Egretta garzetta

Identification: Length 56 cm. Small slender all white heron with black legs and yellow feet and a long thin black bill. In the breeding season it has a long wispy crest.

Voice: Various croaking calls.

Local Status: Found in rocky coastal areas and roosts in trees.

Grey Heron *Ardea cinerea*

FACT FILE

Common Name: Grey Heron

Latin Name: Ardea cinerea

Identification: Length 90 cm. Large, pale grey above and white below with a black crest from the eye and around the neck. Often seen standing or wading in shallows.

Voice: Croaking and rasping at the nest and a loud harsh 'frarnk' in flight.

Local Status: Wetlands of all kinds, inland and especially on the coast.

FACT FILE

Common Name:	Brent Goose
Latin Name:	Branta bernicla
Identification:	Length 56-61 cm. A small goose with black head, neck and breast, with small white marks at the side of the neck, a white rump and black legs. Feeds on marine vegetation like eel-grass.
Voice:	Soft croaks and growls.
Local Status:	Winter visitor to many island bays. A regular flock commutes between Herm and Belle Greve Bay.

Greylag Goose *Anser anser*

FACT FILE

Common Name:	Greylag Goose
Latin Name:	Anser anser
Identification:	Length 76-89 cm. Big, greyish brown, pink legs and orange bill. Feeds on grasses and vegetation.
Voice:	Loud nasal honking.
Local Status:	A local feral population is widespread on pastures and is especially common on the Colin Best Nature Reserve.

Mallard *Anas platyrhynchos*

FACT FILE

Common Name:	Mallard
Latin Name:	Anas platyrhynchos
Identification:	Length 58 cm. The drake is largely grey with a glossy green head, white collar, yellow beak and brown breast. The duck is pale mottled brown. A surface feeder up-ending in search of submerged vegetation.
Voice:	The duck has a loud quack and the drake a quieter high pitched call.
Local Status:	Guernsey's commonest duck, with a large feral population.

FACT FILE

Common Name:	Wigeon
Latin Name:	Anas penelope
Identification:	Length 46 cm. The male is grey with a brown head, yellow forehead, pinkish breast and white belly. The female is reddish brown with a short neck and rounded head. Feeds entirely on vegetation in shallows or by grazing.
Voice:	Low quiet note and male has a loud whistle.
Local Status:	Small flocks overwinter in wetlands such as the Claire Mare.

FACT FILE

Common Name:	Teal
Latin Name:	Anas crecca
Identification:	Length 35 cm. The drake has a brown head with a broad green stripe from the eye, a white band along its side and a cream and black undertail. The duck is mottled brown with pale cheeks and a dark crown.
Voice:	A high grating quack.
Local Status:	Found in small numbers in wetland habitats including seasonally flooded areas.

FACT FILE

Common Name:	Shoveler
Latin Name:	Anas clypeata
Identification:	Length 51 cm. The drake is mostly white with a bottle green head, chestnut belly and flanks and large dark beak. The duck is like a small mallard but with a large beak pointed downwards while swimming.
Voice:	The drake has a low double note.
Local Status:	Mainly marshland but scarce on local wetlands.

Shelduck *Tadorna tadorna*

FACT FILE

Common Name:	Shelduck
Latin Name:	Tadorna tadorna
Identification:	Length 61 cm. Large, mainly white with blackish green head and wing, with a chestnut band around the forepart of the body. Feeds on marine molluscs, crustaceans and worms.
Voice:	Nasal quacks and most vocal during the breeding season.
Local Status:	There is currently an increasing population and pairs can be found in many local bays.

FACT FILE

Common Name: Buzzard

Latin Name: Buteo buteo

Identification: Length 51-56 cm. Medium to large raptor with broad wings and short rounded tail. Mainly brown above and paler below, tail closely barred with dark band at the tip.

Voice: Clear plaintive mewing.

Local Status: Wooded areas and open farmland.

Sparrowhawk *Accipiter nisus*

FACT FILE

Common Name:	Sparrowhawk
Latin Name:	Accipiter nisus
Identification:	Length 28-38 cm. Small hawk with rounded wings and long tail. The male is blue grey above and closely barred orange below. The female is much larger than the male and is brown above and barred brown below.
Voice:	Rapid 'kek-kek-kek' and various loud mewing noises.
Local Status:	Mainly woodland and gardens.

FACT FILE

Common Name:	Marsh Harrier
Latin Name:	Circus aeruginosus
Identification:	Length 48-56 cm. Long winged and long tailed hawk. The male is dark with a paler head and red brown underparts.
Voice:	High pitched calls during breeding, otherwise silent.
Local Status:	Found on marshes and reed beds, and nearby open country.

Kestrel *Falco tinnunculus*

FACT FILE

Common Name:	Kestrel
Latin Name:	Falco tinnunculus
Identification:	Length 34 cm. Most common falcon, often seen hovering. The male has a grey-blue head and tail and a chestnut back spotted with black. The female is larger, chestnut brown above and a barred darker tail with a small dark moustache like stripe.
Voice:	Shrill 'kee-kee-kee' when breeding.
Local Status:	Our commonest bird of prey, found in all areas.

Pheasant *Phasianus colchicus*

FACT FILE

Common Name:	Pheasant
Latin Name:	Phasianus colchicus
Identification:	Length ♂ 66-89 cm and ♀ 53-63 cm. Distinctive male with mottled browns, greys and golds, bottle green head, red eye wattles and long pointed tail. The female is duller pale mottled brown and has a shorter tail.
Voice:	The male has a loud crowing 'korr-kok' and the female a quieter thin whistle.
Local Status:	Introduced by local gun clubs and now increasing in numbers.

Water Rail *Rallus aquaticus*

FACT FILE

Common Name:	Water Rail
Latin Name:	Rallus aquaticus
Identification:	Length 28 cm. Secretive, small and slender bird with a long red bill. Brown above with darker streaks, a blue-grey face, throat and underparts and strongly barred black and white flanks.
Voice:	Distinctive 'gep-gep-gep' grunts and squeals and wild pig like scream.
Local Status:	Dense waterside vegetation, especially marshes. More often heard than seen.

Moorhen *Gallinula chloropus*

FACT FILE

Common Name:	Moorhen
Latin Name:	Gallinula chloropus
Identification:	Length 33 cm. Common waterbird, mainly blackish upperparts with a white horseshoe under the tail and white stripe along the flanks. A red and yellow bill and long greenish legs.
Voice:	Varied sharp single notes, 'prr-ook' or 'kittick'.
Local Status:	Virtually all freshwater habitats.

FACT FILE

Common Name:	Coot
Latin Name:	Fulica atra
Identification:	Length 38 cm. All black rounded body with white bill and frontal crown and long greenish legs.
Voice:	Various sharp notes like, 't-kowk', 'pik' and 'tewk'.
Local Status:	Open water, reservoirs and larger ponds.

FACT FILE

Common Name: Oystercatcher

Latin Name: Haematopus ostralegus

Identification: Length 43 cm. Distinctive, large black and white wading bird with white wing bars, long orange bill and pink legs.

Voice: Noisy loud 'kleep-kleep' and a loud 'pic-pic-pic'.

Local Status: Common on all coasts.

Lapwing *Vanellus vanellus*

FACT FILE

Common Name:	Lapwing
Latin Name:	Vanellus vanellus
Identification:	Length 30 cm. Metallic greeny-black above, black breast, white belly and chestnut undertail. Long wispy crest and distinctive black and white wings.
Voice:	Loud 'pee-wit' call.
Local Status:	Variable numbers overwinter on farmland and marshes.

FACT FILE

Common Name:	Ringed Plover
Latin Name:	Charadrius hiaticula
Identification:	Length 19 cm. Small plover, light brown above and white below. White wingbars, white forehead, collar and stripe behind the eye. Black cheek patch and breast band, orange-yellow legs.
Voice:	Pleasant 'too-leep' and a trilling 'quitoo-weeoo'.
Local Status:	Muddy and sandy shores, especially Vazon Bay and Grand Havre.

FACT FILE

Common Name:	Grey Plover
Latin Name:	Pluvialis squatarola
Identification:	Length 28 cm. Larger round headed plover. Summer plumage is silver-grey above and mottled black below bordered white. In winter very pale brownish-grey above and whitish below. Short dark bill, a large dark eye, greyish legs and conspicuous black mark under the wings.
Voice:	Rather mournful triple call, 'tlee-oo-ee'.
Local Status:	Found in small numbers in all bays.

Turnstone *Arenaria interpres*

FACT FILE

Common Name:	Turnstone
Latin Name:	Arenaria interpres
Identification:	Length 23 cm. Small robust wader with short bill. In summer, brown and black above with black and white head. In winter dark brown above. White below with patterned black and white wings and orange legs.
Voice:	Sharp rattling and trilling notes.
Local Status:	Common winter visitor and migrant found on most beaches, often in small flocks.

FACT FILE

Common Name:	Snipe
Latin Name:	Gallinago gallinago
Identification:	Length 27 cm. Black and brown above with pale stripes and some white on the tail. A long dark bill, short legs and a striped crown.
Voice:	Rasping single and a repeated 'chick-a, chick-a'.
Local Status:	A winter visitor and migrant found on freshwater marshes.

Curlew *Numenius arquata*

FACT FILE

Common Name:	Curlew
Latin Name:	Numenius arquata
Identification:	Length 53-58 cm. Large wader streaked greyish-brown with whitish belly and rump with very long downward curved bill.
Voice:	Loud 'coor-lee'.
Local Status:	A common wader found on many beaches. Often roosts in flocks on the Colin Best Nature Reserve.

FACT FILE

Common Name:	Whimbrel
Latin Name:	Numenius phaeopus
Identification:	Length 41 cm. Resembles the Curlew but smaller and has a shorter downward curved bill. Streaked greyish-brown and with two broad, dark crown stripes with a pale stripe in between.
Voice:	Distinctive high whistling notes.
Local Status:	A migrant species found in several coastal areas and occasionally overwinters here.

Bar-tailed Godwit *Limosa lapponica*

FACT FILE

Common Name:	Bar-tailed Godwit
Latin Name:	Limosa lapponica
Identification:	Length 38 cm. Long legged wader with a long straight bill. Head and breast is chestnut with flanks and belly, whitish in winter and tail barred.
Voice:	Low pitched 'karrat' call in flight and a shrill 'krick' of alarm.
Local Status:	Small numbers of this migrant overwinter in local bays.

FACT FILE

Common Name:	Common Sandpiper
Latin Name:	Tringa hypoleucos
Identification:	Length 20 cm. Olive-brown above and on the breast, white underparts and white wing bars. Constantly bobbing head and tail when on the ground.
Voice:	Piping 'twee-see-se' and high, rapid 'titti-weeti, titti-weeti'.
Local Status:	A passage migrant mainly associated with freshwater areas.

Redshank *Tringa totanus*

FACT FILE

Common Name:	Redshank
Latin Name:	Tringa totanus
Identification:	Length 28 cm. Brown above and closely streaked underparts. White rump and rear edges to the wings. Red bill with dark tip and bright orange-red legs.
Voice:	Very noisy, high pitched 'tleu-hu-hu' and an insistent 'teuk-teuk' when alarmed.
Local Status:	A winter visitor to local beaches.

FACT FILE

Common Name:	Dunlin
Latin Name:	Calidris alpina
Identification:	Length 17-19 cm. Common small wader. In summer chestnut brown above, paler below with a black belly. In winter more pale and grey with a white belly. Dark, slightly down curved bill, dark legs, rump and tail.
Voice:	Short high 'treee' and a long whirring trill.
Local Status:	Prefers sandy beaches such as Vazon and Grand Havre.

Sanderling *Calidris alba*

FACT FILE

Common Name:	Sanderling
Latin Name:	Calidris alba
Identification:	Length 20 cm. Small plump active wader which races along the seashore and chases retreating waves. In winter is very pale grey above and in summer has chestnut upperparts and white below. Short dark bill.
Voice:	Short 'twick'.
Local Status:	Small flocks can be seen in many bays.

FACT FILE

Common Name:	Great Skua
Latin Name:	Stercorarius skua
Identification:	Length 58 cm. Like a large gull in shape but dark brown to black with black legs and bill and white patches across the base of the primaries.
Voice:	A harsh 'skeeerr' and short barking notes.
Local Status:	Usually, only seen at sea or during seawatches.

FACT FILE

Common Name:	Great Black-backed Gull
Latin Name:	Larus marinus
Identification:	Length 64-79 cm. Very large gull with dark black back and wings with flesh coloured legs and heavy yellow bill.
Voice:	Loud and guttural 'kee-ow, kee-ow, kee-ow'.
Local Status:	Common resident.

Lesser Black-backed Gull *Larus fuscus*

FACT FILE

Common Name:	Lesser Black-backed Gull
Latin Name:	Larus fuscus
Identification:	Length 53-56 cm. Slate grey wings and back and yellow legs. Like the Herring Gull, the immature birds are mottled brown and grey.
Voice:	Deep and loud 'kee-ow, kee-ow, kee-ow'.
Local Status:	A common summer visitor and migrant.

FACT FILE

Common Name:	Herring Gull
Latin Name:	Larus argentatus
Identification:	Length 56-66 cm. Larger than the common gull with heavier bill and flesh coloured legs. The bill has a red spot. Immature birds are mottled brown and grey.
Voice:	Loud 'kee-ow, kee-ow, kee-ow'.
Local Status:	Common and widespread resident.

FACT FILE

Common Name:	Black-headed Gull
Latin Name:	Larus ridibundus
Identification:	Length 35-38 cm. Lightly built gull. In summer has a dark brown head and in the winter the head is white with a grey mark behind the eyes.
Voice:	A harsh 'kraar'.
Local Status:	Common gull which leaves the island for a 12 week period to breed.

Sandwich Tern *Sterna sandvicensis*

FACT FILE

Common Name: Sandwich Tern

Latin Name: Sterna sandvicensis

Identification: Length 41 cm. Large white tern with long wings and forked tail. Shaggy black crown, black legs and black bill with yellow tip.

Voice: Grating 'kee-rit'.

Local Status: Fairly common summer visitor and migrant on coasts. Also winters in small numbers.

FACT FILE

Common Name: Common Tern

Latin Name: Sterna hirundo

Identification: Length 35 cm. Graceful, slender seabird with long tail streamers. Mainly white below and pale grey above with a black crown and a white forehead in winter. The bill is red with a black tip.

Voice: A long 'kree-errr, kirr-kirr' and a sharp 'kik-kik-kik-kik'.

Local Status: Fairly common summer visitor to coastal areas and occasionally breeds here.

Razorbill *Alca torda*

FACT FILE

Common Name:	Razorbill
Latin Name:	Alca torda
Identification:	Length 41 cm. Black head and upper parts. Thicker build than the Guillemot with a heavier bill, a white vertical line across the middle and a white line running along the bill to the eye.
Voice:	Various growls and whistles during breeding.
Local Status:	Uncommon resident.

Guillemot *Uria aalge*

FACT FILE

Common Name:	Guillemot
Latin Name:	Uria aalge
Identification:	Length 42 cm. Penguin like with a long pointed bill. Black above and white below and some have a white spectacle around the eye.
Voice:	A harsh 'aaaarrr' at breeding grounds.
Local Status:	Fairly common resident seabird, more numerous around Herm and Sark.

Puffin *Fratercula arctica*

FACT FILE

Common Name:	Puffin
Latin Name:	Fratercula arctica
Identification:	Length 30 cm. Black above and white below with grey-white cheeks. Unmistakeable in summer with its large, wedge shaped, multi-coloured bill which is smaller and grey in winter.
Voice:	Various growling notes.
Local Status:	Found in colonies on cliffs and coastal areas around Herm, Sark and Alderney.

Rock Dove or Feral Pigeon *Columba livia*

FACT FILE

Common Name:	Rock Dove or Feral Pigeon
Latin Name:	Columba livia
Identification:	Length 33 cm. A wide range of colours but the genuine wild Rock Dove is blue-grey with a pale back, a white rump and two black bands across the wing.
Voice:	Cooing 'oo-roo-coo'
Local Status:	Common and widespread. Breeds on cliffs and in towns.

Stock Dove *Columba oenas*

FACT FILE

Common Name:	Stock Dove
Latin Name:	Columba oenas
Identification:	Length 33 cm. Dark blue-grey with a pinkish neck patch.
Voice:	Monotonous 'ooo-roo-oo'.
Local Status:	Found on farmland and scattered woodland.

Woodpigeon *Columba palumbus*

FACT FILE

Common Name: Woodpigeon

Latin Name: Columba palumbus

Identification: Length 41 cm. Large mainly grey with a white patch at the side of its neck, a white band across the wing and a dark band on the tail. Pinkish neck and upper breast.

Voice: Five syllable cooing emphasised on the first.

Local Status: Common across the islands, increasingly in gardens.

Turtle Dove *Streptopelia turtur*

FACT FILE

Common Name:	Turtle Dove
Latin Name:	Streptopelia turtur
Identification:	Length 27 cm. Smaller than the Collared Dove, sandy-brown above with black markings, a pinkish throat and breast and white below.
Voice:	A purring 'roo-rrr'.
Local Status:	Now a scarce summer visitor in woodland and farmland.

Collared Dove *Streptopelia decaocto*

FACT FILE

Common Name:	Collared Dove
Latin Name:	Streptopelia decaocto
Identification:	Length 32 cm. Small pale pinkish-grey dove with a long tail and a black collar.
Voice:	Monotonous 'coo-coo-coo'.
Local Status:	Widespread throughout urban and country areas.

Barn Owl *Tyto alba*

FACT FILE

Common Name:	Barn Owl
Latin Name:	Tyto alba
Identification:	Length 34 cm. Nocturnal hunter, white face with black eyes. Pale golden with white underparts and long legs. Feeds on small mammals, small birds and insects.
Voice:	Long eerie shriek.
Local Status:	Found across the island, usually seen over farmland.

FACT FILE

Common Name: Swift

Latin Name: Apus apus

Identification: Length 16.5 cm. Black all over with long scythe shaped wings and a short forked tail.

Voice: Noisy shrill screams and screeches.

Local Status: A widespread summer visitor, breeding in buildings.

Kingfisher *Alcedo atthis*

FACT FILE

Common Name:	Kingfisher
Latin Name:	Alcedo atthis
Identification:	Length 16.5 cm. Squat with a large head and long dagger shaped bill and short tail. Brilliant electric blue-green above with a cobalt streak along its back. A white throat and neck patches and a chestnut belly.
Voice:	A piping 'chee' or 'chee-chee'.
Local Status:	A non breeder found around reservoirs, ponds and sometimes along the seashore.

Sand Martin *Riparia riparia*

FACT FILE

Common Name:	Sand Martin
Latin Name:	Riparia riparia
Identification:	Length 12 cm. Smallest European Martin. Brown above, white below with a band across the breast.
Voice:	High pitched 'tirrip'.
Local Status:	A common migrant, occasionally breeding in soft cliffs.

FACT FILE

Common Name: House Martin

Latin Name: Delichon urbica

Identification: Length 12.5 cm. Like the Swallow but with shorter wings and tail. Blue black above and white below with a distinctive white rump.

Voice: High chirrups and a simple twittering song.

Local Status: A fairly common summer visitor, breeding under the eaves of buildings.

FACT FILE

Common Name:	Swallow
Latin Name:	Hirundo rustica
Identification:	Length 19 cm. Slim long wings and long streamers on the tail. Dark blue-black above and white below with a dark blue band at the throat and chestnut forehead and chin.
Voice:	Rapid twitters and various liquid calls.
Local Status:	A common migrant but declining breeder. Often nests in accessible barns and sheds.

Meadow Pipit *Anthus pratensis*

FACT FILE

Common Name:	Meadow Pipit
Latin Name:	Anthus pratensis
Identification:	14.5 cm. Olive brown with small dark streaks and pale brown breast.
Voice:	A plaintive 'seep', a single high note as the bird climbs ending in a long trill as it descends.
Local Status:	An uncommon breeder on coasts and commons. Widespread on migration.

Rock Pipit *Anthus petrosus*

FACT FILE

Common Name:	Rock Pipit
Latin Name:	Anthus petrosus
Identification:	16.5 cm. Large dark streaked olive green pipit with grey outer tail feathers and dark legs.
Voice:	A thin 'seep' or 'seep-eep' less musical than the Meadow Pipit.
Local Status:	Scattered coastal resident, more common in winter.

Yellow Wagtail *Motacilla flava*

FACT FILE

Common Name:	Yellow Wagtail
Latin Name:	Motacilla flava
Identification:	Length 16.5 cm. Yellow underparts and green back and the head and neck varies - yellow or grey.
Voice:	A loud mellow 'tseep' and simple song 'tsip-tsip-tsipsi'.
Local Status:	Found on farmland and coasts on migration.

Common Name: Grey Wagtail

Latin Name: Motacilla cinerea

Identification: Length 18 cm. Very slender, blue grey above, bright yellow under a long black tail. Male has a yellow breast in summer.

Voice: A sharp 'chiz-eet'.

Local Status: Uncommon winter visitor, found around streams and the reservoir.

FACT FILE

Common Name:	Pied Wagtail
Latin Name:	Motacilla alba
Identification:	Length 18 cm. Slender grey above and white below. The male has a black back and bib in summer.
Voice:	Double note 'che-sweep', 'chissick'.
Local Status:	Common winter visitor, often around coasts.

Starling *Sturnus vulgaris*

FACT FILE

Common Name: Starling

Latin Name: Sturnus vulgaris

Identification: Length 21.5 cm. Black plumage with a purple-green sheen, spotted with white (especially in winter).

Voice: Wide range of whistles, rattles and clicks. A great mimic.

Local Status: Widespread resident, very common in winter.

Magpie *Pica pica*

FACT FILE

Common Name:	Magpie
Latin Name:	Pica pica
Identification:	Length 46 cm. Distinctive black and white plumage and very long tail.
Voice:	Harsh 'chak-chak-chak'.
Local Status:	Common and widespread resident.

FACT FILE

Common Name:	Jackdaw
Latin Name:	Corvus monedula
Identification:	Length 33 cm. Black plumage apart from grey at the back and sides of the head.
Voice:	High 'chack' and 'kyaa' notes.
Local Status:	An uncommon resident found on open farmland.

FACT FILE

Common Name:	Carrion Crow
Latin Name:	Corvus corone
Identification:	Length 47 cm. Large all black plumage, bill and legs.
Voice:	Harsh 'kraaa'.
Local Status:	Common and widespread resident.

Raven *Corvus corax*

FACT FILE

Common Name:	Raven
Latin Name:	Corvus corax
Identification:	Length 64 cm. Large wholly black with massive bill. Much larger than the crow with longer wedge shaped tail. Will eat a wide range of animals, plant food and carrion.
Voice:	Distinctive deep croak, 'prruk-prruk'.
Local Status:	Scarce resident, found mainly on inaccessible cliffs.

Dunnock *Prunella modularis*

FACT FILE

Common Name:	Dunnock
Latin Name:	Prunella modularis
Identification:	Length 14.5 cm. Streaked brown upperparts, grey head and grey below with darker streaks along its sides.
Voice:	Sweet warble.
Local Status:	Common and widespread in gardens, parks, woodland and scrubby areas.

Wren *Troglodytes troglodytes*

FACT FILE

Common Name:	Wren
Latin Name:	Troglodytes troglodytes
Identification:	Length 9.5 cm. Common tiny brown rotund bird with a short tail held upright. Has a pale eyestripe.
Voice:	A distinctive 'tit-tit-tit' which turns into harsh rattling call when disturbed.
Local Status:	One of the Bailiwick's most common birds, found in many habitats.

Sedge Warbler *Acrocephalus schoenobaenus*

FACT FILE

Common Name:	Sedge Warbler
Latin Name:	Acrocephalus schoenobaenus
Identification:	Length 13 cm. Brown above with streaks and a tawny rump. Whitish stripe over the eye and creamy white below.
Voice:	A sharp 'tuc' and varied with long trills and high chirrups.
Local Status:	Common migrant found in marshes and reedbeds.

FACT FILE

Common Name:	Reed Warbler
Latin Name:	Acrocephalus scirpaceus
Identification:	Length 12.5 cm. Brown above and whitish below. Reddish rump and buff along the flanks.
Voice:	Sharp 'tac' and long song of repeated trills and short phrases.
Local Status:	Common migrant and summer visitor, breeding in reedbeds.

Garden Warbler *Sylvia borin*

FACT FILE

Common Name:	Garden Warbler
Latin Name:	Sylvia borin
Identification:	Length 14 cm. Brown above, pale below and a short bill.
Voice:	Song is similar to the Blackcap.
Local Status:	Scarce summer visitor and migrant. Prefers scrubby areas.

FACT FILE

Common Name:	Blackcap
Latin Name:	Sylvia atricapilla
Identification:	Length 14 cm. Black cap, grey above and paler below. Female is browner with reddish-brown cap.
Voice:	Hard 'tac-tac' and a rich warbling song.
Local Status:	Common summer visitor, nesting in woodland and scrub. Overwinters in small numbers.

FACT FILE

Common Name:	Whitethroat
Latin Name:	Sylvia communis
Identification:	Length 14 cm. The male has a grey cap and a distinctive white throat and pinkish-buff below, rusty-brown wings and long tail. The female is browner.
Voice:	Hard 'check' and short fast warbling song.
Local Status:	Common summer visitor, breeding on cliffs and commons.

FACT FILE

Common Name:	Dartford Warbler
Latin Name:	Sylvia undata
Identification:	Length 12.5 cm. Dark grey head and brown above. Long dark brown tail with white outer feathers. Dark reddish below with white spots on the throat.
Voice:	Slurred 'tchirrr' and musical song.
Local Status:	Scarce but occasionally found in areas of gorse.

Willow Warbler *Phylloscopus trochilus*

FACT FILE

Common Name:	Willow Warbler
Latin Name:	Phylloscopus trochilus
Identification:	Length 11 cm. Pale greenish-brown above and yellow-white below, pale eyestripe and pale legs.
Voice:	Liquid musical song which grows more pronounced and ends with short flourish.
Local Status:	A common migrant.

FACT FILE

Common Name:	Chiffchaff
Latin Name:	Phylloscopus collybita
Identification:	Length 11 cm. Greyish-brown with pale eyestripe and blackish legs.
Voice:	Song is a rising and falling repetition of two calls, 'chiff' and 'chaff'.
Local Status:	Common summer visitor to open woodland. A few overwinter.

FACT FILE

Common Name:	Goldcrest
Latin Name:	Regulus regulus
Identification:	Length 9 cm. Tiny bird, olive-green above and whitish below. Yellow crown with black edging. A large dark eye and narrow dark moustache.
Voice:	High pitched 'see-see-see-see'.
Local Status:	An uncommon breeder and common migrant in mixed woodland and gardens with hedges and conifers.

Firecrest *Regulus ignicapillus*

FACT FILE

Common Name:	Firecrest
Latin Name:	Regulus ignicapillus
Identification:	Length 9 cm. Similar to the Goldcrest but greener above and paler below. White stripe above and a black stripe through the eye.
Voice:	Similar to the Goldcrest but more of a 'zit'.
Local Status:	A common autumn migrant. Some overwinter.

Pied Flycatcher *Ficedula hypoleuca*

FACT FILE

Common Name:	Pied Flycatcher
Latin Name:	Ficedula hypoleuca
Identification:	Length 13 cm. Pied with white underparts, wing patches and forehead. The female is more drab-brown above.
Voice:	Short sharp notes, 'tic', 'weetic' and phweet'.
Local Status:	An uncommon migrant.

Spotted Flycatcher *Muscicapa striata*

FACT FILE

Common Name:	Spotted Flycatcher
Latin Name:	Muscicapa striata
Identification:	Length 14 cm. Grey-brown above and whitish below with a light streaking on the breast and a spotted crown.
Voice:	Thin high 'see' and a quick 'see-tuc-tuc'.
Local Status:	A scarce migrant. Occasionally breeds in wooded areas.

Wheatear *Oenanthe oenanthe*

FACT FILE

Common Name:	Wheatear
Latin Name:	Oenanthe oenanthe
Identification:	Length 14.5 cm. The male is pale blue-grey above with black wings and tail and a pale breast. The female has similar patterns but is pale brown rather than grey. Both have a dark eye patch.
Voice:	Short harsh 'wee-tack'.
Local Status:	Common migrant, particularly on coasts and farmland.

Stonechat *Saxicola torquatus*

FACT FILE

Common Name: Stonechat

Latin Name: Saxicola torquatus

Identification: Length 12.5 cm. Small and plump. The male has a black head, a dark streaked back, reddish breast and white half-collar. The female is reddish-brown.

Voice: A hard 'wheet, sack-sack'.

Local Status: Uncommon resident of commons, coastal areas and heath.

Robin *Erithacus rubecula*

FACT FILE

Common Name:	Robin
Latin Name:	Erithacus rubecula
Identification:	Length 14 cm. Orange-red face and breast, olive-brown above and whitish below.
Voice:	Thin 'see' and a hard 'tic-tic-tic' and a mournful warbling song.
Local Status:	Common in gardens, parks, woods and hedges.

FACT FILE

Common Name:	Blackbird
Latin Name:	Turdus merula
Identification:	Length 25 cm. All black with yellow bill and eye ring. The female is dark brown above and pale mottled brown below.
Voice:	When disturbed a loud 'chink-chink-chink'. Loud warbling song.
Local Status:	Common resident of gardens, hedgerows and woodland.

FACT FILE

Common Name: Redwing

Latin Name: Turdus iliacus

Identification: Length 21 cm. Like the Song Thrush but darker and with streaks rather than spots on the breast. Distinctive broad yellowish eyestripe and chestnut flanks and underwings.

Voice: A thin 'seee' in flight and variable song.

Local Status: A common winter visitor to woodland and open country.

Song Thrush *Turdus philomelos*

FACT FILE

Common Name:	Song Thrush
Latin Name:	Turdus philomelos
Identification:	Length 23 cm. Brown above and white mottled brown below.
Voice:	Sings with loud musical phrases repeated two to four times.
Local Status:	Fairly common in hedgerows, woods, parks and gardens.

Fieldfare *Turdus pilaris*

FACT FILE

Common Name:	Fieldfare
Latin Name:	Turdus pilaris
Identification:	Length 25.5 cm. Pale grey head and rump, dark tail, chestnut back and chest with mottled sides.
Voice:	Harsh 'schack-schack-schack'.
Local Status:	A winter visitor to open woods, fields and pastures, sometimes in large flocks.

Blue Tit *Cyanistes caeruleus*

FACT FILE

Common Name:	Blue Tit
Latin Name:	Cyanistes caeruleus
Identification:	Length 11.5 cm. Green back with blue crown, wings and tail. Yellow underparts, white cheeks and black eyestripe.
Voice:	Commonly a 'tsee-tsee-tsee' and short single 'sit'.
Local Status:	Very common resident found in woodland, hedgerows and gardens.

Great Tit *Parus major*

FACT FILE

Common Name:	Great Tit
Latin Name:	Parus major
Identification:	Length 14 cm. Black head with white cheeks, greenish-blue above and yellow below with a broad black stripe from throat to belly.
Voice:	Commonly 'tsink-tsink' and a ringing 'tee-cha, tee-cha, tee-cha'.
Local Status:	Very common resident found in woodland, hedgerows and gardens.

Long-tailed Tit *Aegithalos caudatus*

FACT FILE

Common Name:	Long-tailed Tit
Latin Name:	Aegithalos caudatus
Identification:	Length 14 cm. Tiny bird with very long tail. Pink-brown, white and black plumage with a whitish head and dark stripe above the eye.
Voice:	A sharp 'tupp', 'tsirrup-tsirrup' and a high 'zee-zee-zee'.
Local Status:	Fairly common resident found in woodland, hedgerows and gardens.

Short-toed Treecreeper *Certhia brachydactyla*

FACT FILE

Common Name: Short-toed Treecreeper

Latin Name: Certhia brachydactyla

Identification: Length 12.5 cm. Streaked
brown upperparts and white below and
pale stripe over the eye. The fine long
billcurves downward.

Voice: Shrill 'srrieh' and rhythmic
'teet,teet, teeterroit'.

Local Status: Common resident found
in woodland, hedgerows and parks.

FACT FILE

Common Name:	House Sparrow
Latin Name:	Passer domesticus
Identification:	Length 14.5 cm. The male is streaky brown above and greyish white below with a grey crown and rump and black bib. The female paler and browner.
Voice:	Various chirps and twitters.
Local Status:	Common resident in urban areas and in farmland.

FACT FILE

Common Name:	Chaffinch
Latin Name:	Fringilla coelebs
Identification:	Length 15 cm. Common finch. The male has dark wings, a chestnut back and blue-grey crown with large pinkish underparts and a white shoulder patch and wing bars. The female is a paler olive-brown above and lighter below.
Voice:	A cheerful 'chwink' and 'wheet'.
Local Status:	Common and widespread resident found in gardens, parks and woodland.

Bullfinch *Pyrrhula pyrrhula*

FACT FILE

Common Name:	Bullfinch
Latin Name:	Pyrrhula pyrrhula
Identification:	Length 14.5 cm. Black crown and bill. The male is blue – grey above, black wings and rose-pink below. The female is grey – brown above and pinkish-brown below.
Voice:	Soft piping and quiet warbling.
Local Status:	Fairly common resident in gardens, parks and woods.

Greenfinch *Carduelis chloris*

FACT FILE

Common Name: Greenfinch

Latin Name: Carduelis chloris

Identification: Length 14.5 cm. Olive green with yellow wing patches, sides of the tail and rump.

Voice: Long nasal 'sweeee' and a twittering trill.

Local Status: Common and widespread resident found in gardens, parks, woodland and open country.

FACT FILE

Common Name:	Goldfinch
Latin Name:	Carduelis carduelis
Identification:	Length 12 cm. Unmistakable markings with a red face, ringed with white and black. Brown above and pale below with a black tail, and black wings with yellow wing-bars especially striking in flight.
Voice:	Liquid 'deedelit' often repeated.
Local Status:	Common resident in cultivated land and waste ground, gardens and orchards.

FACT FILE

Common Name:	Linnet
Latin Name:	Acanthis cannabina
Identification:	Length 13.5 cm. The male has a greyish head, chestnut back and pinkish breast with red on the crown and breast in summer. The female is browner with no red markings.
Voice:	A single 'tsooeet' and a long twittering song.
Local Status:	Fairly common resident found in open country, farmland and coastal areas. Often in flocks in winter.

Snowy Owl *Lihou Island*

Less common species and occasional visitors to the islands of Guernsey, Alderney, Sark and Herm

On the following pages you will find a list of birds that can be found on the islands but are not currently considered to be common birds of the Bailiwick. As changes in land use and climate affect the local environment the bird populations of the islands have altered. Some species are thriving and some are declining in numbers. Birds like the Yellowhammer, which were once considered common, are now just occasional visitors, whereas, the Little Egret was once a rare visitor that generated great excitement but is now a common sight along the west coast. In addition to this list there are well over 100 rare species that have visited the islands and an impressive selection are seen each year. Among these are Black Storks that were spotted over St Sampsons, Guernsey and a Snowy Owl that took up residence on Lihou Island for several months. There is always the chance that you might spot something rare and interesting here in Guernsey, Alderney, Sark and Herm.

Enjoy your bird watching on the islands.

RED-THROATED DIVER *Gavia stellata*
Rare winter visitor to bays

BLACK-THROATED DIVER *Gavia arctica*
Scarce winter visitor to bays

GREAT NORTHERN DIVER *Gavia immer*
Uncommon winter visitor to bays

RED-NECKED GREBE *Podiceps grisegena*
Rare winter visitor to bays

SLAVONIAN GREBE *Podiceps auritus*
Uncommon visitor to bays

BLACK-NECKED GREBE *Podiceps nigricollis*
Rare winter visitor to bays

SOOTY SHEARWATER *Puffinus griseus*
Uncommon autumn visitor offshore

MANX SHEARWATER *Puffinus puffinus*
Fairly common visitor offshore

BALEARIC SHEARWATER *Puffinus mauretanicus*
Uncommon visitor offshore

STORM PETREL *Hydrobates pelagicus*
Fairly common offshore

BITTERN *Botaurus stellaris*
Rare visitor

GADWALL *Anas strepera*
Scarce winter visitor

PINTAIL *Anas acuta*
Scarce winter visitor

Uncommon Visitors

GARGANEY *Anas querqueula*
Scarce spring migrant

POCHARD *Aythya ferina*
Scarce winter visitor

TUFTED DUCK *Aythya fuligula*
Uncommon resident

EIDER *Somateria mollissima*
Rare winter visitor

COMMON SCOTER *Melanitta nigra*
Uncommon migrant offshore

RED-BREASTED MERGANSER *Mergus serrator*
Scarce winter visitor in bays

GOOSANDER *Mergus merganser*
Rare winter visitor

HONEY BUZZARD *Pernis apivorus*
Scarce migrant

HEN HARRIER *Circus cyaneus*
Rare migrant

OSPREY *Pandion haliaetus*
Scarce migrant

MERLIN *Falco columbarius*
Uncommon winter visitor

HOBBY *Falco subbuteo*
Uncommon migrant

PEREGRINE *Falco peregrinus*
Uncommon resident

RED-LEGGED PARTRIDGE *Alectoris rufa*
Introduced

GREY PARTRIDGE *Perdix perdix*
Introduced

AVOCET *Recurvirostra avosetta*
Rare visitor

LITTLE RINGED PLOVER *Charadrius dubius*
Uncommon migrant

DOTTEREL *Charadrius morinellus*
Scarce migrant

GOLDEN PLOVER *Pluvialis apricaria*
Uncommon winter visitor and migrant

KNOT *Calidris canuta*
Uncommon winter visitor and migrant

LITTLE STINT *Calidris minuta*
Rare migrant

CURLEW SANDPIPER *Calidris ferruginea*
Uncommon migrant

PURPLE SANDPIPER *Calidris maritima*
Scarce winter visitor

RUFF *Philomachus pugnax*
Scarce migrant

JACK SNIPE *Lymnocryptes minimus*
Scarce winter visitor and migrant

WOODCOCK *Scolopax rusticola*
Common winter visitor

Uncommon Visitors

BLACK-TAILED GODWIT *Limosa limosa*
Uncommon migrant

GREEN SANDPIPER *Tringa ochropus*
Uncommon migrant

SPOTTED REDSHANK *Tringa erythropus*
Rare migrant and winter visitor

GREENSHANK *Tringa nebularia*
Uncommon migrant

WOOD SANDPIPER *Tringa glareola*
Scarce migrant

GREY PHALAROPE *Phalaropus fulicarius*
Scarce migrant and winter visitor

POMARINE SKUA *Stercorarius pomarinus*
Scarce migrant offshore

ARCTIC SKUA *Stercorarius parasiticus*
Uncommon migrant offshore

KITTIWAKE *Rissa tridactyla*
Uncommon visitor

LITTLE GULL *Hydrocoloeus minutus*
Rare winter visitor and migrant

MEDITERRANEAN GULL *Larus melanocephalus*
Uncommon migrant and winter visitor

COMMON GULL *Larus canus*
Uncommon winter visitor

YELLOW-LEGGED GULL *Larus michahellis*
Scarce visitor

LITTLE TERN *Sternula albifrons*
Rare migrant

BLACK TERN *Chlidonias niger*
Rare migrant

ARCTIC TERN *Sterna paradisaea*
Scarce migrant

CUCKOO *Cuculus canorus*
Mainly uncommon migrant

LONG-EARED OWL *Asio otus*
Uncommon resident

SHORT-EARED OWL *Asio flammeus*
Scarce winter visitor and migrant

HOOPOE *Upupa epops*
Rare migrant

WRYNECK *Jynx torquilla*
Scarce migrant

GREAT SPOTTED WOODPECKER *Dendrocopos major*
Mainly scarce visitor

SKYLARK *Alauda arvensis*
Uncommon winter visitor and migrant

RICHARD'S PIPIT *Anthus richardi*
Rare migrant

TAWNY PIPIT *Anthus campestris*
Rare migrant

TREE PIPIT *Anthus trivialis*
Uncommon migrant

BLACK REDSTART *Phoenicurus ochruros*
Uncommon migrant and winter visitor

REDSTART *Phoenicurus phoenicurus*
Uncommon migrant

WHINCHAT *Saxicola rubetra*
Uncommon migrant

RING OUZEL *Turdus torquatus*
Uncommon migrant

MISTLE THRUSH *Turdus viscivorus*
Uncommon migrant and winter visitor

CETTI'S WARBLER *Cettia cetti*
Scarce resident

GRASSHOPPER WARBLER *Locustella naevia*
Scarce migrant

MELODIOUS WARBLER *Hippolais polyglotta*
Rare migrant

LESSER WHITETHROAT *Sylvia curruca*
Scarce migrant and summer visitor

YELLOW-BROWED WARBLER *Phylloscopus inornatus*
Scarce autumn migrant

WOOD WARBLER *Phylloscopus sibilatrix*
Scarce spring migrant

BEARDED TIT *Panurus biarmicus*
Rare visitor

COAL TIT *Periparus ater*
Scarce autumn and winter visitor

Snow Bunting *Fort le Crocq*

Uncommon Visitors

GOLDEN ORIOLE *Oriolus oriolus*
Rare spring migrant

BRAMBLING *Fringilla montifringilla*
Uncommon winter visitor and migrant

SERIN *Serinus serinus*
Scarce visitor

SISKIN *Carduelis spinus*
Uncommon migrant and winter visitor

LESSER REDPOLL *Carduelis cabaret*
Rare migrant and winter visitor

CROSSBILL *Loxia curvirostra*
Scarce visitor

LAPLAND BUNTING *Calcarius lapponicus*
Scarce autumn migrant

SNOW BUNTING *Plectrophenax nivalis*
Uncommon migrant and winter visitor

YELLOWHAMMER *Emberiza citrinella*
Rare visitor

ORTOLAN BUNTING *Emberiza hortulana*
Rare autumn migrant

REED BUNTING *Emberiza schoeniclus*
Scarce migrant and winter visitor

Thanks to Jamie Hooper and Paul Hillion
for their help, advice and enthusiasm.
Their expert local knowledge has been
invaluable in putting this book together.

Thank you to all the photographers who
willingly contributed their photographs
to this book:

Paul Hillion
Barry Wells
Chris Bale
Steven Round
Rod Ferbrache
Vic Froome
Carolyn Brouard
Mike Cunningham
John Robinson
Mick Dryden

The rights to the images contained
in this book belong to the individual
photographers. They may not be
reproduced or redistributed without
prior permission.